MODEL FAMILIES

SHIRLEY A. SERVISS

Rowan Books

Canadian Cataloguing in Publication Data
    Serviss, Shirley Ann, 1953-
    Model Families

    Poems
    ISBN 1-895836-02-6

    1. Family – Poetry. I. Title.
PS8587.E777M6 1992 C811.54 C92-091811-5
PR 9199.3.S47M6 1992

Cover design by Kathryn Hines

Typesetting by Black Type: White Paper

Printed and bound in Canda by
Signature Press Inc., Calgary

Rowan Books Limited is an imprint of
The Books Collective
214-21-10405 Jasper Avenue
Edmonton, Alberta
T5J 3S2

Telephone: (403) 454-3233

*T*o Richard
the father
of both my children

Acknowledgements

Some of the poems in this collection have appeared in the following magazines: *Grain, Cyphers, Orbis, The New Quarterly, CV2, HERizons, Secrets from the Orange Couch, Other Voices*, and *The Newsmagazine by Alberta Women*. Many of the poems have been broadcast on CBC Radio on *Alberta Anthology* and performed in Celebration of Women in the Arts' *Womanstrength* and *Fringe* productions. One of the poems was performed in *Starwords* (1989 National Book Week presentation).

Thanks go to the Alberta Foundation for Literary Arts for the grant which bought me the time to write a good portion of this collection, to Rudy and Tena Wiebe for the nurturing environment of Strawberry Creek Lodge where much of the collection was written and to Lorna Crozier who edited my manuscript at the Sage Hill Writing Experience in Saskatchewan.

Appreciation is also extended to the following poets and friends who provided constructive criticism during the revision stage: Bert Almon, Florence Cockwill, Margaret Cunningham, Marian Daugela, Peggy Dodson, Ruth Donovan, Candas Jane Dorsey, Gordon Fearn, Leona Gom, Amber Hayward, Gerald Hill, Alice Major, Nancy Mattson, Rhona McAdam, Mary McDonald, Beth Munroe Hill, Margaret Ellen Peach, Norm Sacuta, Debbie VanKeeken, and Janeen Werner-King.

one

Preservation

The cold room in her parents' cellar holds
shelves of pickled carrots, sealers of canned
crabapples, raspberry jam in old mayonnaise jars.
Onions tied with bindertwine hang from the low ceiling.
Two freezers are filled with roasts wrapped in brown
paper, homemade bread in plastic bags, apple pies
in foil stacked in soda biscuit boxes.

The cupboards in her city apartment are bare
but for a few tins of asparagus, crabmeat and mushrooms.
Her fridge holds nothing but yoghurt, coffee, and
sometimes white wine. "We called you Saturday night,"
her mother would say on the phone, "and before
church Sunday morning." *I'm sorry you missed me,*
she has learned to say rather than offer explanations.

Once, she had married to please them, but her marriage
changed in unexpected ways like potatoes sprouting
too soon for spring, grew mould like black
currant jam, rotted like pumpkins.
Now she doesn't know what the future has in store,
can't anticipate meeting her needs with dill pickles,
or Mason jars filled with pears.

Still, when she visits at Christmas,
she packs a pudding made from suet in her suitcase
to take back to the city.

❖

Sons and lovers

My lover is the father of a son
a single parent with spaghetti sauce
on the shoulders of his coat,
cracker crumbs and used Kleenex
in his pockets. He comes courting
with bouquets of chrysanthemums,
a high chair, spare diapers,
a child who throws forks at the walls,
tantrums in public places.

My lover is the father of a son
who goes to bed early. We go to bed
early, explore each other with touch,
with tongue, tell our stories
late into the night. Morning comes
too soon   our sleep disrupted
by a small boy with cold feet,
a runny nose, squirming in
between us.

❖

Living together

Gregory isn't sure he likes me living
with his Dad. He doesn't get his turn
to sleep in his Dad's bed, curled against
his Dad's back. Instead is sent back to his own
bed in the middle of the night. Three-year-old
Gregory would like to sleep with me, too,
would like to sleep between us.

He likes my wind-up musical clown,
likes to have it living in his Dad's house,
likes my donkey with the nodding head.
"Can I keep the donkey when you move
into your own house?" he asks.

Gregory cries for his Mom when I get
shampoo in his eyes. He says his Mom doesn't
put raisins in her pancakes, doesn't have
a mustache like me. He wonders
why I've started to lock the bathroom door.

❖

Finding my place

I'm just the Woman-He-Sleeps-With
says the Mother-Of-His-Child

What am I to the small boy
who snuggles on my lap playing

Snakes and Ladders on a board
I have drawn for him

with buttons from my sewing box
marking our places

❖

Wicked stepmother

She had always seen herself
becoming the bride of the prince
but never contemplated
him coming encumbered
with a child   What a surprise
to hear herself saying
Clean up your plate
or I'll cook you for dinner
Get back into bed or
I'll lose you in the forest

She had never imagined competing
with the real mother   mirrored
in the child's mannerisms
held up as the image of perfection
in the child's mind
never thought she'd find herself
wishing she could hire a woodcutter

The mother-in-love with the child's
father needs a new role to play
where she rescues him
from the gingerbread house
drives him to the ball
(daycare would do) gets to say
I love you which she only dares
to whisper beside his sleeping head

❖

Past~life therapy

What goes around comes around
around we go   two women
in a circle game   circle dance
one step forward   two
steps back   two left feet
one foot in the mouth
Nothing comes out right

What karma must we play
out   this time around
How did I wrong you
in that other life
to make you cast me
as the villain   always wrong
always in the wrong

What would it take to make
things right   If I regress
would I discover I was the
soldier who murdered your mother
the thief who stole your silver
If it would do any good
I confess   I confess

❖

Three times lucky

In Toronto on holiday with me
he tries to call his first wife
There are some things he'd like
to say now   he couldn't then
but none of the numbers are right

The old friends we meet for drinks
like me at least as well as his first
wife and more than the second
his mother keeps wanting
to discuss with me   undeterred
by my noncommittal replies

I'm the third wife he's brought home
to this room where he once studied
math   the third to share his bed
loving silently so the creaking
floors won't give us away
Three times lucky   he tells me
believing he's finally solved the equation

❖

Ties

My stepson is learning
to tie his yellow laces
around the legs of kitchen chairs,
as I used to do, underfoot
on my mother's tiled kitchen floor.

He helps me make Rice Krispie squares,
the recipe written in my childish hand
on scribbler paper, yellowed now,
stirs the melted marshmallows
with a wooden spoon, pats the cake
into the buttered pan.

Putting him to bed, I fan the sheets
up and down, the cool air
kissing him goodnight the way
my mother used to
tuck me in when I was ill.

I'm mothering from memory,
playing by ear, learning the skills
I need to be a parent
as he crosses one lace over
the other, pulls it through.
We're mastering knots
before we move on to bows.

❖

Goodnight gregory

Tonight when you come home
late from your meeting
will you come into my room
and give me a kiss and whisper
"goodnight gregory?" in my ear?

Tonight when I come home
late from my meeting
you'll be sleeping in your other bed
in your other house.
I'll blow a kiss into the night air
and say "goodnight gregory"
to the stars.

Will you forget?

I won't forget. Will you
feel my kiss float
through your window
and land on your cheek?
Will you hear my whisper
in your sleep?

Will you remember me?

❖

two

My unborn poems

My unborn poems
are kicking again tonight
struggling against the limits
of my mortality.

Sensing their immaturity
I hesitate to bear them, yet fear
they will be slowly strangled
by the umbilical cord
of my reserve.

❖

Conception

You were conceived in my mind
on a kinnikinnick-covered ridge
overlooking the mountains
part wish   part prayer
fusing into possibility

You were conceived in my body
on a cold night when northern lights
danced across the sky
a spirit drawn to earth
by the sparks our love kindled

❖

Prenatal musings

I thought there would be time to play
music, relax and feel you move
inside me. In theory that same music
would later soothe you, settle you to sleep.

Instead, I tap my computer keys,
send you messages to wait until
I meet my deadline   a major project
due the same day as you.

I pray the whine of my printer
will have the same effect as Bach.

❖

dream poems

i dream i am changing
the baby and it has legs
like a grasshopper

i dream the sun explodes and the earth begins
to shift until i am alone
on a small sliver of land that breaks
away and drifts into the ocean

i dream a girl baby who smiles
at me and whispers i love you
as she slips through my hands

i dream my elderly mother gives birth
gives the baby to me to look after

i dream of my sister
whose daughter did not survive
her birth

i don't ask my sister
if she dreams of me

❖

Shirley A Serviss

Relativity

This child I can kiss at will
without risking rejection

This child will never say
"She's not my mother"

This child   no one can ever
accuse me of trying to steal

❖

Real mothers

"Your second?"
They eye my bulging
belly as we stand
on the sidelines. Sun slants
across the soccer field.

"My first." They stare
at the small blond
boy in goal. "My stepson,"
I explain. "You'll be a real mother
soon," I'm told. They hold
the hands of smaller children,
scold the ones who stray.

He's playing defense
when he's kicked in the shins,
carried from the field by the coach.
"Do we have a mother here?"

I hesitate, then finally come
forward, claim the sobbing
child, hug the hurt away.

❖

Old wives tales

I was born on Friday the thirteenth. The clock
fell off the wall in the delivery room
and nearly hit my mother on the head.
This is the only funny story
I ever heard her tell about childbirth.

My mother's stories were background music.
Conversations with the hired man's wife
filtered into my world of paper dolls
on the kitchen floor. Babies died of convulsions,
smothered in their mother's beds, fell
down the stairs on their heads,
had hare lips, club feet, arrived stillborn.

She didn't like it when I babysat my cousins.
I stood still beside their beds to listen
to them breathe, placed all the money I earned
in the collection plate Sunday morning
in thanks they had lived through the night.

My mother didn't want us to have babies.
"What did you go and do that for?"
she asked my sister (married thirteen years).
"You're too selfish to have children,"
she told me over and over, "too career-minded."

She phoned as I left for the hospital,
felt my labour pains a province away.
"I'll pray for you," she told me.
"Just don't have any more."

❖

The tree of Diana

Women wanting babies worshipped
Diana   Roman goddess of forest
and groves

Expectant women clasped
the Swedish ash
to ensure an easy delivery

Maternity clothes made from bark
delivered women of the Congo
from the dangers of child bearing

The goddess Latona embraced
two laurel trees as she birthed
Apollo and Artemis

My lover is the tree I lean on
wrap my arms around his trunk
We weather the contractions together

❖

Voyage

It's said the labouring mother
descends into the underworld
fetches a soul to inhabit her child
That's where I spent
those black hours   each push
a plunge into the depths

What an old soul I found
in all that searching

So wise this daughter
wrenched from my body
blue and bruised by the curved blades
cradled around her crowning head

❖

Animal instinct

It's animal instinct
this act of giving birth
of giving up the control
it took us all
these years to learn

We return to the primitive
squat on our haunches
moan and grunt
our bodies sweaty
from our labour

It shouldn't surprise us
when we feel an urge
to lick our offspring
clean

❖

Afterbirth

My doctor shows us the afterbirth
dark blue with blood. I do not think of eating
the placenta or burying it and planting a tree
or saving the cord for a teething ring.
I do not think of ritual, am deprived of the
expected baby at my breast. My baby, blue, bruised
and bloody whisked away while my doctor
tries to stitch me together again.

There is This, This, and, This wrong
with your baby I am told by a strange
pediatrician on waking to a curtained bed
in a strange room. I milk myself
with a machine, saving each precious drop
for the battered baby I stare at through glass,
trying to find a resemblance
among the tubes and wires
a connection after birth.

❖

Cutting ties

The last time I called
my former husband was to say
I'd had a baby. He didn't advise me
of the birth of his son
some years later with a name
I didn't even know   he liked.

Perhaps he has other
unannounced children by now
this man who told me
he didn't want to be a father.
I don't know how to forgive
him for changing
his mind.

He didn't mail me a change
of address when he bought the
land we'd always dreamed
of owning. I didn't phone
when we holidayed
a short drive away.

I've come to respect the
distance he's put between us.
I've no desire to haunt
his marriage, hurt his new
wife with my memories, no wish
to know how much she is
unlike me.

❖

Castoffs

For nearly nine years
she was my mother
shared confidences over coffee
graced my home with her handiwork
made me feel like a daughter
not just the wife of her son

I didn't realize how difficult
it would be to lose a mother
how I would dream of her
years after I had exorcised
the clothes she made me
from my closet   long after
I gained another mother
in her stead

I kept the last sweater
she knit for me   large and loving
hanging almost to my knees
buttoned it over my pregnant
belly   wrapped myself in its
warmth to nurse my baby
the grandchild
I wanted so badly to give her

❖

three

When the wind blows

The summer you were born
the clouds turned green
and the wind blew
babies into the air

The snow did not fall
all that winter and in the spring
no rains came   just storms
of dust rolling across the sky

When you were born
my baby   the world
changed

❖

When the bough breaks

A fine line I walk
in the wakeful hours
of the night   Baby fights
sleep in my arms

Her eyes screwed tightly
shut   she croaks   claws
at my neck   my breast

Shattered awake too many
times in the middle of dreams
Eyes too bleary to make out
the time on the clock
I rock her in aching arms
try to keep from
shaking her to sleep

❖

Incarnation in outer suburbia

She had never imagined
finding herself exiled to outer
suburbia, looking at a moonscape
of barren lawns, remembering
trees that arched above the streets.

She did not know what she was
to do here and watched
the neighbours from her windows
for clues. Accordingly, she put her baby
in an umbrella stroller and pushed her
around the block.

Sometimes the women parked
their strollers in front of one of the houses
and she tried that too, timed her walks
to pass by casually as they sunned on the steps,
older children riding trikes or running
through sprinklers. But she did not know
what to say after the teeth had been counted,
after the introduction of solids.

She saw them cleaning windows, shaking mats,
but such a fate seemed too terrible
to contemplate and she buried herself
in her daily paper in the middle of the living room
floor in a muddle of toys. Some things were
expected, she discovered. He liked to come home
to order and had suddenly become

❖

less able to provide it, leaving in the mornings
a litter of cereal boxes, empty bowls and spoons.
Every afternoon at four she hid the dirty dishes
in the dishwasher, thawed something for supper
in the microwave, sometimes even combed her hair.

The neighbours put their children into their cars,
disappeared for hours at a time, but where
did they go with newborns and two-year-olds?
She finally got brave enough to ask. "Shopping,"
they said as though it should have been obvious.
Shopping. Each day she made a list and saved
excuses for outings: stamps, bagels,
disposable diapers (she would atone
in her next life   come back as a tree).

She overcame her resistance to The Mall,
strolled through its domed streets
stuffing broken shreds of muffin
into her baby's bird-mouth as she bought
children's clothes on her VISA
she would return on some pretext
another day, another expedition out.

❖

Shirley A Serviss

Code

He passed his Morse code exam
the day I brought her home
tunes in to Radio Moscow, the BBC
Deciphers dits and dahs
refracted off the ionosphere

I try to interpret
the tone of her squawks
listen for the faintest
cry from her cradle
change in the rhythm
of her breath

He taps away on his keyer
sending, receiving
rotates his antenna towards
Tokyo, San José, Eskimo Point
turns off the world
and comes to bed

My antennae extends
to the room where she sleeps
On call all day / all night
tuned in to her frequency

❖

She is my lover

She is my lover   Nibbles tenderly
at my nipples   Caresses my breasts
in a proprietary way   Snuggles tight
against my shoulder   Breathes her sweet
breath against my neck

She is my lover   Smiles special
smiles across the room at me
her whole face alight   Reaches out her arms
for me to take her   Fills me with delight
at the feel of her delicate bones
her smooth skin

At night   her father tries
to touch me with his large hands
his rough mouth and tongue   His body
heavy on top of me

At night   too full of her to take another
lover   give in to the pleasure
I used to find in him   My body
torn apart to give her life

❖

Sacrifice

All night my fretful child
fights fever in my arms,
sleeps fitfully, pressed
hot against my chest.

The Armenian woman
trapped in the aftermath of earthquake
pierced her fingers with broken glass,
suckled her child with her blood.

I rock through the dark
hours, stare at my daughter's
moonlit face and know
fear's razor edge.

❖

The psychic link

Nearly everyone has a story

the grandmother who
cried out the moment her son
was killed in battle

the mother who smelled smoke
miles away from home and phoned
to wake her children in the burning house

the father awakened by the crash
of shattered glass as his son broke
into a house on the other side of the city

I wonder if I'll know in time
to warn my daughter not
to catch the plane

❖

Maternal imprinting

Already she has her own life,
gives me a look I can't translate
left in the arms of a stranger.

She comes back to me knowing words
I've not taught her, wearing the scent
of another woman's cologne.

A mother deer would disown her.
I take her home, cover her skin
with kisses to mark her as mine.

❖

Shirley A Serviss

Nature / nurture

I buy my daughter
a rag doll and cradle
for her second birthday.
The doll isn't anatomically correct.
The gift isn't politically correct,
but she has been spending her days
wrapping her toy trucks and tractors
in Kleenex, crooning them to sleep.

I buy my daughter dresses
second hand (even though I swore
she'd wear overalls and jeans),
but she does look sweet in dresses
and I let her get them dirty
playing in the sand.

I nursed my daughter at my computer
(typed with one hand), changed her
diapers on board room tables,
but she loves to bake muffins
carefully places coloured papers
into round holes in the tin.

❖

Shirley A Serviss

Drawing a bath

My daughter brushes blue eyes
on my breasts   curves
a red smile beneath my belly button
her soap paints floating in the tub

I sketch a sun on her tummy
clouds across her chest
I'm painting the world
I want for her

For her I am the world
my smile   the rainbow
promise of gold

❖

Sewing a garden

Sew me a garden, Mom. She brings
my sewing tin, chooses spools
of coloured threads and waits
expectantly. I pray for Rumpelstiltskin
to embroider flowers in the air.

On the last sunny afternoon of autumn
we plant tulip bulbs beside the house,
sow poppy seeds along the neighbour's
fence, cross off the winter days
as we await the magic of spring.

❖

Scars

My daughter cries blood
tears   I try to hold
her still   The doctor stitches
back the corner of her eye
the sutures merging
with her long dark lashes

Dancing   she lost balance
hit the stone hearth
was silent   still   seconds
before the screaming
streaming of blood

My sister at the same age
carrying straw to feed the pigs
stepped on Sandy's sore paw

She wears her scar
beside the same eye
and I the guilt of being there
both times   powerless
to prevent the harm

❖

Hades

Demeter's daughter
disappeared while picking narcissus.
She wandered the world
in search of her,
turning the earth to dust
with her grief.

The day my daughter disappeared
in the world's largest mall
I feared she was forever gone
I screamed her name   turned
back the time   denied I'd turned
away from her one moment
let her from my sight

This time the gods forgave me

❖

Missing in/action

This morning I started a poem   *Athena   born full grown*
still beneath the covers   *her father's daughter*
unwilling to come out   *his head struck open*
into the growing light   *with a double-edged axe*
my daughter teething   *Her golden armour*
on my nipples   warming   *protects her from pain*
her cold hands on my breast   *Nothing distracts her*
I would remember later   *from her destiny*
reciting the words in my mind   *this childless goddess*

A moment of quiet waiting in front of the school
for my son   my daughter asleep in the back seat
my poem vanished along with the day

❖

four

Child splitting

How do you split a child
        split him in two
        split him into what
what are we turning him into
                his mother's baby
                our big boy
                little boy with his poker face
playing his hand
close to his chest
not giving anything
        away

How do you divide a child
King Solomon found the real mother
was willing to give her child up
        to spare his life

Neither parent is willing to give
        him away
give up on the idea
of shared custody
                half the time here
                half the time there
                half the time in his own world

Where does he go
when he closes up

❖

Re~entry

Wish I could greet you with banners,
balloons, your favourite cake.
Instead I make you hang
your coat, take off your shoes.

You come back to us
wearing the manners of your other
house, bearing the baggage of your
mother's life, leaving essentials behind.

I find it hard to accept your
return, try too hard to turn you back
into our son. Wish I could still
my tongue, let you find your own way
home.

❖

Life in the blender

The books I read call us
a blended family. Toss in one
small boy, two homes, three parents
and push all our buttons.

His mother's change of plans,
stir things up. Our rules grate on her.
She tries to turn us to mush
with her threats. We grind her
down with our insistence
on having things our way.

My stepson throws tantrums
in his room, cries for hours
while our small daughter
chops the hair off her doll.

Pour us out in public at the Sunday
service, Meet the Teacher night
and watch us mix and intermingle
smooth as an espresso shake.

❖

Soccer game

Gregory is playing soccer. His real mother
is the one sitting on the cooler in her
long white skirt with her paperback
Making It To The Top. She is
sitting on my cooler talking to my
husband who was once her husband
and is the father of her son.

Gregory is playing soccer. It is his turn
to bring snack. His real mother didn't rush
to Safeway to buy oranges and watermelon.
She didn't cut up oranges and watermelon,
make supper, dress Gregory in his uniform,
change his half-sister's diaper and find her shoes
so we could all go to the game.
She took the day off, she tells my husband,
and read in the sun.

Gregory is playing soccer. I am chasing
his small half-sister along the sidelines
trying to keep her off the field. I am wearing
spat-up oranges on the shoulder of my t-shirt.
His mother is reading *Making It To The Top*,
sitting on top of my cooler in her long white skirt,
talking to my husband, while I am picking seeds
out of my daughter's watermelon
and the juice is running all over my cut-off jeans.

Gregory is playing soccer. No one is keeping score.

❖

Model families

My husband is interested in topology.
He says it's a way of overcoming
false boundaries between outside
appearances and inside feelings,
a way of dealing with anything
paradoxical or transcendent.

> Topology: *topos*
> (see TOPIC) + LOGY

I try to apply his need for logic
to the topic of our family,
draw on Venn diagrams
(remembered from high school math)
as a way to help him get the picture.

> Venn diagrams after John Venn
> using overlapping circles
> to show relationships between sets.

We're a family with a twist.
A family with two members who were once
part of another,
part of another circle.

> Circle: Something having the form
> of a circle, as a crown, halo, or ring.

❖

Still, at times, the lines intersect.

A family with two members who are still
part of that other family,
part of her circle.

> Circle: A group of persons united
> by some common interest or pursuit.

Her circle encroaches on mine.
She draws my spouse, my stepson away,
drops by with gifts and birthday
kisses for my husband,
tries to take my daughter:
"Come to *me*, Janelle"
every time she comes in the door,
suggests we name her guardian
in our wills.

> Circle: *Logic* A fault in reasoning
> in which the premise and conclusion
> are each in turn used to prove the other;
> also called *vicious circle*.

❖

At one, Janelle knows who is in
her circle: "Mommy, Daddy, Gregory.
Mommy, Daddy, Gregory" her daily litany.

Letting Gregory into my circle
means including his mother.
He mentions her at every meal,
corrects anyone who dares mistake
me for his mother. If she is Mom
who am I? If she is ex-wife
how long will I be wife?

I draw the circle I want as family:
only the four of us inside.

"You are shutting out reality"

He draws another circle
with her inside. Her circle takes in Gregory,
but leaves his father in mine.
I am no longer tempted
to draw a circle around my daughter
and me   draw away.

❖

We talk about ways to make our circle
more impermeable. We sleep
curled together   a Mobius strip.

> Mobius strip (after A.F. Mobius,
> mathematician)
> a surface with only one side...

❖

step by step

step: derived from the old
English word meaning
bereaved or deprived
The step parent
a replacement
someone who stepped in
to rescue the bereaved family

step: to pass into a situation,
circumstance etc.
as if in a single step
(as in walk down the aisle)

in step: in accord
with the proper rhythm or cadence,
or in conformity with others
out of step: (a stepmother,
an oddity, an extra parent)

to take steps: to adopt
measures as to attain an end
(to discipline, to feed and clothe,
to love, to look for love
in return)

to step down: to decrease
gradually or by degrees;
to abdicate (to stop trying
to please, to help, to rescue,
to step in)

❖

Allegory

My stepson and I read a bedtime
story he brought home from school
about a stepmother so cruel
the children turn her into a toad.

"That's all well and good for the kids,
but what about the poor old king?"
(My skin grows warts even as I speak.)
"The children will grow up, leave home
and he'll be all alone in that big old castle."

He lies awake, waiting for his mother's
promised call. Maybe she can't get the
operator, find a telephone, is still in a meeting.
He gets angry when I suggest he try to sleep.
"She'll call tonight. She said she would."

It would do no good to tell him
the stepmother in stories
is the real mother in disguise.
I feel the poison flowing to my skin,
silence my long, sticky tongue.

❖

The stepfather's story

I wasn't the first man
to marry a woman carrying another's child.
Nor the last. Even in good Jewish families
like mine. Who would have to know?
I thought it would be our secret.
Do you think the angels could keep
their mouths shut? Announcing his birth
to the shepherds: Christ the Lord!

And then the wise men showed up
and the cat was really out of the bag.
Mind you, so was the gold, incense and myrrh
and I have to admit the money came in handy
when we had to flee to Egypt.
Just compensation I figure.
If they hadn't told Herod, we could have
gone back to Nazareth where I had a good
name as a carpenter.

You think it's easy living
in a blended family? Especially in these
shared custody situations
when the other parent wants a voice
in the decisions. And He'd never talk
directly to me. Always sending angels
with messages   directives from on high.
It's lucky I can read
the writing on the wall.

❖

It's tough being a stepfather
especially when the boy's real Dad
is the Almighty
authority on everything.
I make furniture, build houses.
God made heaven and earth,
and do you think He'd let me forget it?

I tried to be easy on the boy
give him a break. A stepfather can afford
to be a bit indulgent. It's no reflection on me
how the kid turns out. His real Father
was a bit hidebound, I thought
all those "thou shalts" and "shalt nots."
But Jesus had a self-righteous streak
in him too. "That's not how things are done
in my Father's house," he'd say,
as if I gave a carpenter's damn.

I taught him everything I knew
how to mortise a corner, drive a nail,
measure everything twice.
A guy needs to earn an honest living,
but you just can't fight heredity.
He had this fascination for sleight of hand:
calming the waves, turning water into wine,
rousting evil spirits. You know the kind of thing
I mean. No money in it, but he built up
quite a following. Just like his real Father.

❖

I warned him he'd come to no good end,
but do you think he'd listen to me,
what with his Father calling him all the time?
I don't have to tell you he broke his mother's heart.
He always was Mary's favourite
firstborn son and all.
As for me, maybe it's just natural
to love your own flesh
and blood more   even though I tried
my level best to be fair.
But it was always "Joseph"
this, and "Joseph" that. I wished
the kid would sometimes call me *Dad*.

❖

Denial

Simon Peter I deny him
this half-son / half brother of my daughter's
who lives with us half the time.
"How many children do you have?"
"One, only one," I say
waiting for the cock to crow.

My revenge for all the years of one
Mother's Day card not addressed to me,
the Christmas present for his
"one and only nicest mom in the world,"
he'll place beneath another tree.

"So, you work in the hospital?"
a new neighbour asks. "No."
"Then you must write poetry.
He tells me he has two mothers
one works in a hospital and the other
is a poet." Forgive me, my son.

❖

The other mother's story

My son has a sister, but she's
not allowed to play at my house,
not allowed to stay for weekends
even though I've offered to keep her,
to let them get away. I know how
kids can tie you down.

She says she doesn't trust me
with her daughter. Just because I swore
at her, made threats: the time my ex
refused to hang my drapes, the time
she turned up at the parent-teacher interview.
Hell that was years ago! Doesn't this woman
have better things to do than carry around
this baggage from the past?
Sure she pissed me off
letting my son call her Mom,
trying to come between us.
I guess I said some things I shouldn't have,
but things are different now.

❖

It was a bitch sharing my only son
with some stranger shacked up
with my ex-husband. Susie Homemaker
playing mother to my four-year-old
for months at a time. Always baking
those damn Rice Krispie squares,
sewing on his Cub badges.
I was scared I'd lose him forever
if you want the truth.

It's not like I'm asking for joint custody
of their kid. I just want my son
to see his little sister.
What does she think I could
possibly do to her precious daughter?
What kind of a mother
does she think I am?

❖

Wanted

Wanted: Sexy stepmother. Good with kids & good in the kitchen. Must be able to handle daily interactions with child's real mother/husband's former spouse. No pay. Yearly vacation with child.

❖

Family vacation

We are on a road called Going
to the Sun, going mad,
the kids fighting in the back seat
brakes (and tempers) overheating.
Hours of gut-wrenching curves
later, we reach Kalispell.

That night over a bottle of wine,
my husband tells me his illusions
have been shattered. We are
a dysfunctional family
he has concluded, after one hot
day cooped up together in the car.

I let him sleep in, keep the kids
quiet, teaching them variations
of Solitaire, plan next year's
vacation   a week alone
somewhere far from Montana.

❖

Positive thinking

Pasting pictures into his photograph
album, I focus on the positive
side of our life together.

My stepson grows from a small boy
in a baseball cap, swinging a plastic bat,
into a toothless swimmer,
his eyes the colour of the pool.

He peers into a microscope,
hammers tent pegs into place,
rides a bike for the first time
wind in his hair, pleasure on his face.

The camera captures the moments
we've chosen to remember:
the spin of the merry-go-round,
the climb to the mountain peak,
lead role in the Christmas play.

I file the negatives away.

❖

five

Wives~in~law

Ours is an unnatural connection
bound together without rules
or traditions   No wonder we don't know
how to behave towards each other

A triangle
rocking from point to point
in a struggle to conduct our lives
Each interaction strikes
a discordant note

Welded together by a mutual husband
for better or worse   'till death do us part
Involuntary kinship to a woman
I did not marry
Our differences repel us
yet the same man held an attraction
the spaces between his teeth
the touch of his hands

I don't want to understand her
reasons for rejecting him   His version
has become my truth   my armour
against her   I'm uneasy
when I catch her eyes   find myself
in harmony

❖

The next step

"You be the mom
and I'll be the stepmom."
My daughter and her friend play
house, find the perfect compromise
both allowed to mother.

My stepson's mom and I learned
this game by trial and error,
had more fights, have never
become friends.
But we're sharing the roles
with more ease   ever since
she too had a chance
to play stepmother.

❖

Rubik's cube

Six years we've twisted and turned
tried different combinations:
half a year here, half a year there;
three months with his mother, three
months with us; alternate weekends;
alternate months with access on
demand   seeking the perfect solution.

The latest twist: one primary
residence   his mother's house
a single colour on one side/two sides/
maybe even three. At last the pieces
fall into place for me   no more contortions
as I try to make it work for all the rest,
see all sides, be what I could never be.

My husband's face of the puzzle
is still out of synch. One piece is
missing from his life: his son.
A weekend once a month
won't fill the space, won't make it right.
All I can do is hold him in the night
his hurt too great to be dis/solved by tears.

❖

Ghost pain

For him it is a missing
limb   this loss of his son
this too-early amputation
A part of him severed
from his example of heart
and muscle that make a man
The pain a constant
reminder

He feels his son's ghost presence
his empty place at the table
his empty room at the end
of the hall   his ball glove
discarded by the back door

Worse is the emptiness
inside him   the stillness
in place of all the wisdom
he had to share   He is haunted
by the things he left unsaid

His hope is that the many
nights he left meetings
to skip stones in the river
walk in the ravine
work on times tables
will speak for him

❖

Sympathetic magic

Corn mother   last sheaf
made large and heavy
to secure a good harvest
                      the coming year
thrown into the river
to ensure rain

What expectations we have
of our mothers
how badly we treat them
                again and again
how badly we need them

Corn Mother fertilizes the crops
withers them up
                when she's angry

❖

Her father's eyes

Ma-ma Ma-ma this baby
knows my name *Ma-ma Ma-ma*
looks at me with her father's eyes
Blue eyes   Sometimes focused on me
filled with love   Sometimes
unseeing   taking-for-granted
eyes   the same as her father

This baby born with long
narrow feet   Her father's feet
kicking against my rib cage
all those months inside me
All those months of thinking
she was *my* baby   Born a stranger
not mine at all   Her father's daughter

Ma-ma Ma-ma it is my mother too
I take for granted   My mother I complain to
My mother I expect to take me as I am
It is my father I look like   look up to
Ma-ma Ma-ma forgive me
for trying so hard not to be like you
for all the times I've
kicked you in the heart

❖

Like my father

I am a mother like my father
haunting my daughter's nights.
I stare at her still form
        hold my breath
                until I hear her breathe
and remember my father
                silhouetted in the moonlight
retrieving quilts
I had shucked off in sleep.

I am a mother like my father
        more comfortable with silence
                than with speaking.
I sing to my daughter
        the songs he yodelled
as we bumped along
gravel roads in his Fargo truck.

I am a mother like my father
        awake at every cough
        concerned by every fall.
You'll hurt yourself
comes quickly to my tongue.
I have to teach myself to say,
Jump, my daughter.   Run.

❖

The alphabet / backwards

He was always older than other kids'
fathers   as old as their grandfathers
but young enough to ride my first bicycle
to the barn   balancing a milk pail
in each hand

When I turned eight he bought me
roller skates at the auction   adjusted
them to fit his boots   skated in the hayloft
on a path he cleared between the bales
scaring the cows

Now he walks with a cane as slowly
as my daughter toddled her first steps
rests on my spare bed in the afternoons
but is teaching her to say the alphabet
backwards

❖

Shirley A. Serviss

Full circle

My father shaves his white whiskers
into the sink. Still in his flannelete
pajamas, shares the bathroom
with my daughter who has to go pee.

The toenails at the ends of his naked feet
curl up like the hooves of foundered horses.

Once it was difficult for me
to bend around the mound of my belly
to shave my legs. I think of his
arthritic joints, his eighty years.

I have grown accustomed
to the intimacy of caring for others
(*Wipe my bum, Mom*),
have struggled to clip the tiny nails
of my squirming child.

I chip at my father's toenails
with clippers and scissors. They are thick
and brittle like the horns of cattle,
yellow like old piano keys.

❖

Shirley A. Serviss

Property rights

My daughter presses herself tight
against my chest   traps
me in a tangle of arms and legs
plants wet kisses on my mouth

I remember my own
mother's lush body   her ample lap

How I loved to crawl into bed
beside her in the mornings
snuggle into the hollow warmth
of my father's place
breathing his scent in the sheets

Our daughter waits for daylight
throws herself into our room
tunnels into the space between us
warming her cold feet
in the muff of my pubic hair

❖

Mothers don't make music

In my family   nothing
below the waist has a name.
"Your aunt had her *organs*
removed," my mother tells me
and I imagine men   marching
through my aunt's living room
carrying off her Hammond.

My mother was never comfortable
talking about sex   except to say
"Nice girls don't think
about things like that. Go play
the piano."

Now I'm a mother too
my husband's overtures
don't strike the right chord.

❖

Shirley A. Serviss

Mother nature

In the woods   I am
near you mother
the fermenting scent of dying leaves
cranberry jelly
bleeding through flour sacks
hung from the handles
of your kitchen cupboard doors

      In the woods   I am
      back on summer afternoon
      walks along cow paths
      you pointing out wood violets
      cowslips   calling the trees by name
      I am wading in the creek   mud
      squishing between my toes

In the woods I am mother
hiking with my children
finding pine cones   coloured leaves
prying open rose hips
to show them the waxy skins
that can be boiled for tea
We are picking Saskatoon berries
to turn into pie   I wish
you were here to help me
make the crust

❖

Picking raspberries

1.

I will eat anything
but raspberries

2.

They remind me of too many summer
mornings among spiders and thorns
filling honey pails tied around
my waist with bindertwine
Their seeds   the tears
of self pity I spilled at my child
labour   inventing stories
of possible adoption

3.

At noon   my brother
face blackened by summerfallow
would say he supposed I had been playing
paperdolls   and even my berry-stained
hands could not convince him
otherwise   so sure
his sisters had an easier life

4.

My mother spends her summers   picking
off the small green worms   white
spiders   stray twigs and leaves
boiling the berries into jam
in the close heat of her kitchen
her face polished with perspiration
her apron blemished with their blood

❖

5.
One city summer afternoon
at work with scissors and wax
pasting up a newsletter   my boss
wanders in   "Playing paperdolls?"

6.
My parents tell me on the telephone
they can't come to see me
the raspberries are ready
They should never have had daughters
only raspberries

7.
My daughter picks raspberries
on summer holidays at Grandma's
A novelty for a city child   I think
but she complains about
the boredom   the bugs

8.
My mother sends us home
with raspberry jam
for my husband
It leaks all over my suitcase
gilding the pages of my books
with juice

❖